The Weather Within

Bonnie Michael

BookLeaf Publishing

India | USA | UK

Presentation by *BookLeaf Publishing*

Web: www.bookleafpub.com

E-mail: info@bookleafpub.com

ISBN: 9789363316942

First edition 2024

ACKNOWLEDGEMENT

I would like to dedicate my words to the wonderful people in my life who have played an important role in crafting who I am today.

PREFACE

In a world that often demands stoicism and strength from men, the depths of their emotional lives often remain uncharted territory. These poems are an exploration of that hidden landscape, a cartography of the heart that dares to venture beyond the surface.

Here, you will find verses that echo with the full spectrum of human experience – from the exhilarating peaks of love and joy to the shadowed valleys of grief and despair. There are poems that wrestle with anger and fear, that celebrate tenderness and vulnerability, that grapple with the unspoken anxieties and yearnings that reside within every man.

This collection is an invitation to step into a world where masculinity is not defined by silence or suppression, but by the courage to feel deeply and honestly. It is a testament to the power of poetry to give voice to the unspoken, to illuminate the shadows, and to reveal the profound beauty that lies within the emotional lives of men.

May these poems resonate with you, challenge
you, and ultimately remind you that to be human
is to embrace the full spectrum of our emotions,
in all their complexity and wonder.

The Price of Living a Life of My Own

Another place, another time,
Another thought, that isn't mine.
Everyday amidst a million crimes,
Trapped in an invisible cell, just like a mime.

They say I should love this life on hire,
Slave to life's needs, chanting 'what may I do
sire'.
No voice of my own, no dreams to follow,
Just playing it safe, swimming where it's
shallow.

What happened I wonder, to the spirit of the free
man,
The quests of an adventurer, setting sail without
a plan.
What happened to waking up under a different
sky each day,
Greeting a total stranger by the road and asking
him the way.

Our worlds seem to have shrunk, we live by a
box these days,
Believing all that it shows, trusting all that it
says.
Our thoughts now belong to those the world
calls wise,
We are too scared to think, let alone act without
advice.

And yet we boast of being human, the smartest
of our kind,
Sitting within our cages, no better we will ever
find.
And thus we choose to live the illusion of a lie,
That life was meant to be this way, why be
different, why even try!

But now I am tired of being what the world
wants me to be,
I will no longer ask your permission, I will just
dare to be me.
The rules I follow will be the ones that I make,
My road, my journey, my dreams I will not
forsake.

So go ahead and judge me, look at me through
your crooked lens,
I am kicking down those boundaries, no more
sitting on the fence.
And at the end of my journey, I know I may
stand alone,

Well so be it then, if that be the price of living a
life of my own!

Questions for a Beloved

What if you don't know me
What if when you try,
What if I take off all my masks
What if that makes you cry?

What if you STILL love me
And wish to walk by my side,
What if then the storms of my life
Drag you into high tide?

What if you STILL love me
And years pass by,
What if someone then asks you
Was it worth loving this guy?

What if you then look back
What is it you would see?
Would it be worth all that precious love
Or just life's tragedy?

What if the latter you consider
Is what I now fear,
For I'd rather be someone all alone
Than hurt someone so dear.

The Frosted Garden

A cold wind still blows,
As the rusty old lamp-post still stands,
In the garden crafted in nature's glass,
In a heart that no one understands.

Frosted are the roses,
Frosted is the tree of the lark.
Frosted is that lonely bench,
By that frosted lake in that park.

Winter here … seems to last forever,
Time out here seems to stand still.
Life amidst all this still seems to go on,
Believing that spring shall not pass by again,
Believing still… at least until.

Special Biscuits

As the sun sets into the sea of time,
bringing this day to an end.
I stand in the Kitchen of Memories,
baking a batch of special biscuits for my friend.

It has taken a lifetime to create this recipe,
Each ingredient carefully selected by me.

These are special biscuits, not heavy on the hip,
Baked in the oven of the heart, from the batter of
friendship.

These biscuits are rare, although their flavors are
few,
Strawberry, Chocolate and Mint just for you.

Strawberry, this flavor, will remain for a while,
Reminding you of sweet memories, bringing you
a smile.

Chocolate and milk, a combination so
wholesome,
Gifting you wishes and prayers for the days to
come.

And Mint promises that on a cloudy day, if no
friend you find,
Just turn around, I'll be two steps behind.

And so as the sun sets into the sea of time,
Bringing this day to an end.
I stand in the Kitchen of Memories,
Baking a batch of special biscuits for you,
my friend.

Silence Speaks

Silence, how sweet are your words,
Sweetness not found even in the sound of the
birds.

But not always do we hear you speak,
For you ask for the ears of one who is humble
and meek.

Even the deaf can listen to the words you say,
You talk to us through night, you talk to us
through day.

Within you are hidden the mysteries we try to
find,
Mysteries left unsolved by the human mind.

We are too caught up in the river of life,
Swimming through sorrow, struggling through strife.

We are so ignorant to the wisdom you wish to give,
Help us to listen, teach us to live.

So that when we may rise to the light of a new day,
We may find you as a guide to show us the way.

Tears

Tears, dear tears, tell me why do I cry?
Why, at the slightest grief, you glitter in my eye.

When I am very happy you glow with a smile,
You fill my heart with memories that last more
than a while.

But sometimes I wonder where do you go,
Maybe to some place about which we will never
know.

Or do you, deep down in our hearts hide,
And with the flow of smiles or sorrow with our
words abide.

Tears, please be there in the corner of our eye,
And flow for someone, someday, when I die.

The Man in My Mirror

As I look at the mirror, from the world I feel so
apart,
They say I am a crazy man, I think from my
heart.
Little instances across the day, things that should
not even matter,
Are things that trouble me, and so they call me
Alice's Mad Hatter.
I wish I could talk to this man in the mirror, he
just stands there looking tall,
I'd like to give him a piece of my mind and tell
him I don't like him at all.

He makes me feel attached to people I care,
He tells me it's good your thoughts with friends
to share.
He tells me that to live life as your own, as it
never will happen again,

He tells me to be me, and all such advice, that
always causes me heartache and pain.
And that's when he's silent, when I am much
hurt, that's when he never keeps score,
What do I do when I'm being me and no one
wishes to hear me anymore?
I wish I could talk to this man in the mirror, he
just stands there looking tall,
I'd like to give him a piece of my mind and tell
him I don't like him at all.

He looks back at me, no words does he say, just
stares back into my eye,
A single drop of glitter rolls down his cheek, he
still tries to smile and not cry.
And through that drop as I look back at him, a
different image I see,
He is no stranger that I never met before, he's
just the real me.
The world doesn't like him for he's not that
much fun, they feel he is quite apart,
For they think he is crazy, for he thinks only
from his heart.
I cannot change this world, so I guess for some
time, I'll lock him and keep him away,
Hoping that the world will like to know that man
in the mirror someday.

A Special Day in Love

Life seemed long, but the day was new,
Dreams a many, with hopes though few.

I woke up at the chime, and wondered while I
lay,
Why do I feel this way, is there something
special about today?

And then it struck me, Oh how could I forget?
It's the 8th of January - You guys are still
clueless, I bet!

Well don't seem surprised with that look on your
face,
Only to me is this day special from all the other
days.

It's exactly 3 years since I met that special
someone,
The love of my life, who made life so much
more fun.

With moments to share, with someone beloved
who cares,
To hold someone's hand, a magic only few
would understand.

To love that special woman, and to be loved
back in return,
Are blessings from above that every young heart
would yearn.

And so I got off my bed, there's lots to prepare,
Being late is not for today, I'd rather not dare.

Let's pick her up from work, by 4 should be
fine,
A movie, a walk through the park, and a sweet
place to dine.

She loves pink roses, and chocolates and wind
chimes,
But most of all, she always says, is together
spending some time.

But just then my eyes went to the cracked
photo-frame by the door,
Of when she walked out, saying she loved me no
more.

Oh that's something that just slipped my mind,
Of moments that hurt, of a life left behind.

A single drop of tear, glistens beside my coffee
cup,
It's just another day again, the sun's on his way
up.

Ready for work, and out of the door,
Hoping to find that someone to love once more.

All in a Day's Work

Life seemed long, but the day was new,
Dreams a many, with hopes though few.

I woke up in my bed, last night's vodka still in
my head.
All efforts once again in vain, the clock said I'd
be late to work again.

Off from my home, through rickshaws and
buses,
Packed like sardines in local trains with a crowd
of thousand fusses.

Walking into office planning what's today's
reason to say,
Just to learn that Boss called an early URGENT
meeting today.

The knock at the Board Room door, I could
almost feel the heat,
"Oh so you've finally arrived," says my boss,
my heart skips a beat.

To take your seat and try to gather the crums,
And try to ignore the shady comments from
some of the bums.

2 hours of brain-storming, but yet most of it a
waste.
Decisions are taken based on the last 5 minutes
and that too in haste.

It's lunch time by then, time to grab a bite,
Hustling one's way through the cafeteria frenzy,
It's no less than a fight.

Back to your cubicle, in 20 minutes sharp,
To still find the Big Kahuna standing there, like
a devil with a harp.

5 new plans to implement, in 5 different ways.
And all this needs to be done by the end of the
day.

So I set my schedule, let's get it done by 4,
At 3:40, the Big Guy calls me up to say, "Let's
re think these plans once more".

Back at my desk, a little banging of the feet,
3 hours of dedicated hard work and a SHIFT &
DELETE.

Back in his cabin, new thoughts floating in the
air,
He goes off on his tangents, leaving us pulling
our hair.

The meeting ends a minute before 7,
Which means with these new plans, I'll be
working again till 11.

Walking out of office, back on the train,
Too late for dinner, it's Take Out food once
again.

As I lie on my bed, I hear the street dogs howl,
As I ponder for a few minutes on my lifestyle of
an owl.

Trrriinnggg! Goes the clock, it's another new
day again,
With a hundred new experiences ready to drive
me insane.

But time goes on and it's not all just strife. . .
It's all part of this wacky adventure called—
"The Common Man's Life."

A Wish

I live in troubled times, beyond the myst of
uncertainty.
I live in days of sorrow,
Where tears seem to last an eternity.

In a land of plenty, I hear my brothers sigh!
And through the hoardings of a few,
I see the masses cry.

My neighbour sees me as a threat, he no more
knows my face.
He remembers not the countless moments,
Of joy from our past days.

I walk amidst a crowd of sheep, in others faults I
see.
I wish to live in a world of sight,
Where CHANGE begins with me.

Finding Our Common Day

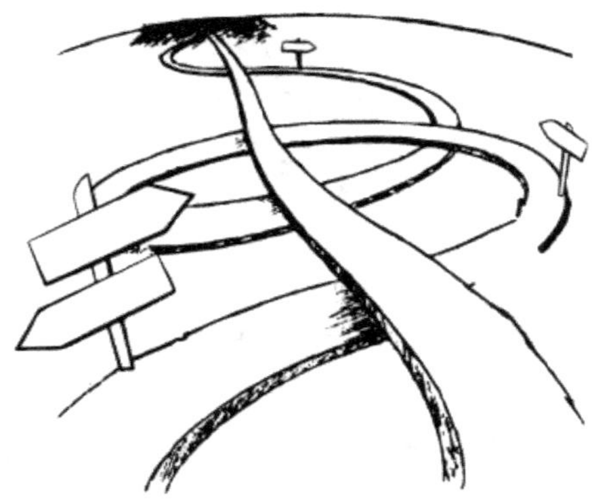

In fire's blaze, cold water's peace I crave,
A cascade's rush, a calming, cool embrace.
Yet in that chill, a fiery warmth I long,
My past like water, future flames belong.

Night's darkest depths hold naught of fear for
me,
Nor day's bright sun too brilliant to see.
Life's fleeting span, a truth I'll never grieve,
While death's embrace forever takes its leave.

In rage's grip, self-answers I pursue,
Yet peace reveals a life not wholly true.
An ordinary man, a life mundane,
Who am I? To you, to me, arcane.

Yet I exist, in life's grand tapestry,
More than survive, in moments' symphony.
A day, they say, life's essence to distill,
Yet lost in hours, time's relentless mill.

My words may stray from reason's well-worn
path,
But your life's course, it mirrors mine in wrath.
In what you have, you seek a wished-for prize,
In what you want, the unattainable lies.

Strange you may seem, yet not unlike I am,
Together flawed, in thought and deed we stand.
We live, we dream, in hopeful faith we trust,
Our flaws transformed, our spirits free from
dust.

Wonderful we are, with hope as our guide,
Though ego's cloak we often wear with pride.
In poverty of self, we claim the world's domain,
Yet closing eyes, the truth we can't restrain.

We are but blind, yet yearn to lead the throng,
Through mists of doubt, our journeys to prolong.
But hope remains, a gift to light our way,
In flawed humanity, we find our common day.

In Rage I lose

In anger's grip I'm held so tight,
A fiery blaze, consuming light.
It burns and sears, a blinding sight,
No friend it sees, no wrong, no right.

It cares not, in its reckless might,
And so in anger, I ignite.

I burn with rage, a molten core,
Volcanic fury, ever more.
No bounds it knows, no guiding lore,
Destroying all that's gone before.

No limits set, no reason sought,
In present rage, all else is naught.
So in this fury, I am caught,
A fearsome force, yet dearly bought.

For in this wrath, I'm weak and frail,
Vulnerable heart, behind the veil.
I act without a thoughtful trail,
My words betray, they often fail.

The damage grows, a bitter cost,
As rage controls, all reason lost.
I am a slave, to anger tossed,
By weakness bound, by fury bossed.

To him who sparks this fiery ire,
In rage's grip, you fan the pyre.
And in this war, I tire and tire,
…In rage and anger, you conspire
…In rage and anger... YOU WIN!!!

The Dreams I Dwell In

A sip of love, my heart's desire,
A taste of truth, a fleeting fire.
A moment's joy, a memory's pyre,
Of sorrow's sting, a love's expire.

I've loved before, and loved again,
More times than two, in joy and pain.
I've felt the touch, so real, so plain,
Yet now it's gone, a phantom strain.

For what was mine, I never held,
To whom I loved, I never dwelled.
A stranger's heart, a tale unfelled,
And in this loss, my soul is quelled.

Oh, love's a jest, a fleeting gleam,
I walk on by, as in a dream.
Yet still I turn, a backward stream,
To glimpse what's lost, in moments between.

They say it's naught, a figment's flight,
But in my world, it burns so bright.
In dreams I dwell, with all my might,
A stranger to today's cold light.

They Say I Have Changed

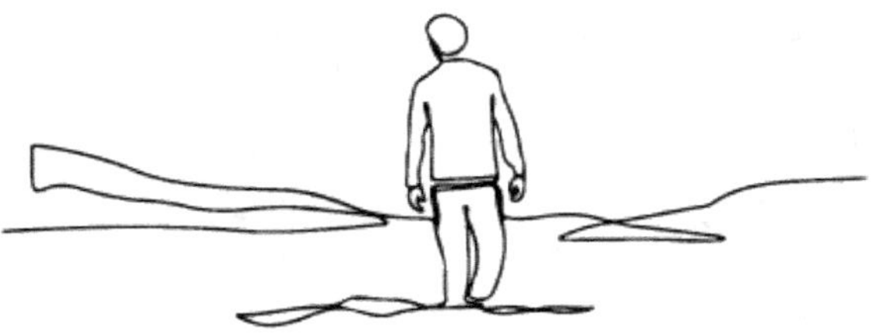

They claim I've changed, these souls who never
knew,
The depths of me, the essence shining through.
They never grasped who I was, nor the path I
pursue,
And who I am, remains forever veiled from their
view.

They say I've shifted, a different person they see,
Yet never glimpsed the one I used to be.
Not for a day, nor a moment's fleeting decree,
Did they truly know the heart that beats in me.

And so I ponder, who has truly transformed?
Or what has shifted, if truth be adorned?
Is it their window, perception newly formed?
Or is it my mask, finally gently warmed?

Has clarity dawned, the fog beginning to fade?
Or time's own mist, a deeper mystery laid?
I cannot tell, the answers remain unweighed,
But do they know, these voices that have
swayed?

They who declare they know me, inside and out,
Yet see but change, a phantom filled with doubt.
Changed, they say, with voices raised in a shout,
But oh, the depths they'll never know about.

A Monologue by the Sea

In moonlit hush, the sea's nocturnal tongue,
A symphony of voices, softly sung.
The wind's quiet breath, a secret gently hung,
While darkness drapes the sky, where stars are
strung.

The waves' crescendo, a tempestuous plea,
While moonbeams dance, with playful revelry.
A night of whispers, for the soul to see,
In nature's theater, a grand soliloquy.

Oh, silent be, and listen to the night,
Where stillness speaks of dreams beyond our
sight.
The dark reveals the self we hide from light,
A masked facade, concealed from prying sight.

The angry surge, of longings unfulfilled,
Like waves that touch the shore, then gently
stilled.
The moon's coy game, by shadows softly filled,
A lover's chase, in secrets sweetly spilled.

Speak to me, Night, as by the sea I sit,
Tomorrow's dawn, my memory will submit.
Beneath time's sands, my presence it will flit,
So speak to me, before our paths are split.

Oh, Night, converse, while stars above us gleam,
For with the morn, we'll part, as in a dream.
And strangers we shall be, it would seem,
Lost in the echoes of this moonlit theme.

Living by My Heart

They say I'm crazy, a mind unsound,
In this world, this time I've found.
They claim I don't belong, they confound,
These souls who've never truly known me, nor
astound.

They wish to label, to confine, to bind,
Yet never sought the depths within my mind.
But still their words, a chilling wind, they find,
Those trapped in shadows, afraid to leave
behind.

But to myself, I question deep,
Is it I who's mad, or they who sleep?
For eyes they have, yet never truly peep,
Beyond themselves, their secrets darkly keep.

Their ears but hear the greedy coin's cold ring,
Their selfish tongues, no song of kindness sing.
They live to breathe, yet joy does never spring,
Dust in the wind, forever wandering.

Yet I am mad, they say with scornful glance,
Because my heart, in warmth does softly dance.
I see a world, a loving, hopeful trance,
Where souls connect, in life's eternal dance.

But cold I feel, when sorrow fills the air,
A lonely soul, a burden hard to bear.
I share the pain, the heartache and despair,
Of those unwanted, lost in life's unfair.

I shiver too, at futures bleak and grim,
The child who toils, the dreams that start to dim.
The forgotten stranger, a silent, tragic hymn,
A world of pain, where shadows grow so grim.

I laugh at vows, so empty and untrue,
Of peace on Earth, a vision lost from view.
Yet hope remains, a spark that glimmers
through,
The human spirit, yearning to renew.

I still believe, though others call it mad,
In selfless acts, the kindness to be had.
A drop of caring, in hearts grown cold and sad,
To nurture roots, where goodness can be clad.

Yes, this is why they label me insane,
They fear the light, that shines through all my
pain.
They say I'm lost, in life's chaotic strain,
But who's truly lost, when hearts forget to reign?

I question still, with spirit soaring high,
Are my inquiries wrong, or answers just passed
by?
For not all souls with empathy can fly,
In a world where hearts have often learned to
die.

The Page That Changed the Story

What worth my life, if none recall my name,
When morrow comes, and fades my fleeting
fame?
Do I exist, a whisper in the air,
To vanish soon, as though I never was there?

Each thought, each word, each stroke upon life's
art,
Mere lines in sand, soon blown apart?
No, fate like that, my soul cannot impart,
I shall not fade, within time's shadowed heart.

This life, a gift, a clay within my hand,
To mould and shape, by my own will's
command.
A vessel forged, where opportunities expand,
Each drop it pours, will nourish all the land.

For I am not, an ordinary soul,
Nor dwell within a world where shadows stroll.
I walk amongst the few, with purpose bold,
A unique flame, a story yet untold.

Never before, nor ever shall there be,
Another soul, quite like the one in me.
I was designed, for all the world to see,
A destiny, that sets my spirit free.

So why then fade, into the yesteryear,
Amongst the crowd, where dreams dissolve in
fear?
To merely be, a bystander held near,
No, such a fate, I shall not hold so dear.

For I am destined, mark my words this day,
To be that page, where history holds sway.
The chapter turned, where tales forever stay,
The one who changed the story, come what may.

My Journey

Sometimes the path grows dark and drear,
As through scorched fields I persevere.
Dreams shattered, scattered far and near,
Tears of salt, their sorrows sear.

The heart, a burden, heavy weighs,
With chains of grief, from bygone days.
Yet onward still, my spirit sways,
The horizon calls, where sunlight plays.

With gentle neigh, a steed, called Hope,
Consoles my soul, as onward I elope.
Toward my journey's end, I swiftly cope,
The wind now whispers, as I bravely grope.

By streams of thought, I pause to rest,
Hope and traveler, both equally blessed.
Refreshed, renewed, I face the final test,
The path ahead, a clearer view confessed.

A fork appears, a choice to make with care,
What's liked or wanted, paths diverge there.
One road lies open, sunlight in the air,
The other veiled, in mists of foggy lair.

Yet, instinct guides, where logic cannot tread,
Through misty woods, my journey onward led.
The path winds on, unknowns lie ahead,
My quest continues, through fears unsaid.